Stressformers

Stressformers
101 Instant Stress Relief Strategies

Al Jackson

Copyright © 2012, Al Jackson

All rights reserved. No part of this book may be reproduced, stored, or transmitted by any means— whether auditory, graphic, mechanical, or electronic—without written permission of both publisher and author, except in the case of brief excerpts used in critical articles and reviews. Unauthorized reproduction of any part of this work is illegal and is punishable by law.

ISBN 978-1-105-76098-3

I would like to dedicate this book to several people:

To my loving wife, partner and best friend Anisha Jackson, and my children Jalyn and A.J. Jackson. Thank you for loving and teaching me what true joy is.

To my wonderful mother, Rita Jackson. Thank you for loving, mentoring and inspiring me to dream, believe and achieve. I couldn't have made it without you.

To my parents in-law, Alonza and Maxine Holden. Thank you for your constant expressions of love, support and encouragement. We made it together.

To my loving grandmother, Oreatha Ogletree. Thank you for raising us with love and the Keaton family's values.

To my dedicated uncle, Tim Keaton. Thank you for always providing strength for our family and showing me what being a man is all about.

To my father, James Jackson, Sr. Thank you for your love, friendship and telling me how proud you are of me.

To my sister, Tameika Jackson. Thank you for always saying, 'I love and believe in you"

Foreword

When was the last time you were stressed about something? Anything? Probably a few minutes ago right? Maybe even right at this very moment. Well, I want to let you know that you've picked up the right book at the right time, with the right message, written by the right author to help you transform the stress in your life.

Whether the stress you are experiencing comes from work, home, money, faith, family, health, community, online, or anywhere else, the reality is that whatever stress it is.... it's very real and relevant to you.

Al Jackson has done the world a huge favor by creating Stressformers. It is truly a refreshing approach to stress management. I know, because I helped him create it. In this power-packed book, Al has comprised amazing heart-felt personal stories, cutting-edge research, relevant statistics, and most importantly - actionable strategies that will reduce and even in some cases eliminate the stress in your life...starting right now. Loaded with over 101 real, timely and practical techniques that you can implement right away, Stressformers is the type of book that you will be using as a resource for many years to come.

Al's quick-witted one-liners, powerful, punchy action statements, and well-versed perspective on the management of stress will really compel you to live a better overall quality of life as a Stressformer. By the time you finish the first chapter, you will be able to clearly identify the various stressors in your life and how your body currently reacts to them. Furthermore, by the time you get halfway through this book, you should start to feel the shift in your stress levels as you learn to prioritize and effectively process those milestones in your life. On top of that, by the end of this book, I hope that you have made a commitment to living a life of freedom by no longer reacting to the storms of life but rather purposefully deciding how you choose to deal with them.

I am convinced that by the time you finish reading Stressformers, you will be so inspired, empowered, and engaged that you, just like me, will be a champion of this cause. Therefore, your mission, if you choose to accept it, is to take everything that you have learned from reading this book and share these practical principals and strategies with your family, the people you work with, your friends and even a stranger. Let the powerful partnership that you and Al Jackson will form after reading this book be the catalyst that equips you to help those around you break the chains of stress off of their lives. Let's Stressform this world together.

Delatorro L. McNeal, II, M.S. CSP
Performance Strategist, Certified Speaking Professional Best Selling Author of *Caught Between a Dream and a Job*
www.Delatorro.com www.CaughtBetweenADreamAndaJob.com
www.ThrivingThroughYourStorms.com

Contents

Introduction

Congratulations on being stressed out. You may ask why would you make a statement like that? In short, it is because stress and pain are great motivators. According to many experts, pain is a more significant motivator than pleasure. If you think about it, most of the major breakthroughs in human rights, technology, equality and invention have come after seasons of extreme pain. Even the salvation of mankind came through the ultimate pain that was suffered by the Lord Jesus Christ. Therefore, pain can be productive. I believe your past pain can produce your present power. As the old saying goes, "No pain, no gain." I'd like to add, "No scars, no stars." Pain properly channeled can be very productive. Think about a woman, who is pregnant and close to giving birth. The more intense and painful her contractions are, the closer she is to giving birth to a new life. Think about that for yourselves. You have experienced tremendous stress in your life; otherwise, you would have never purchased this book. Think of that stress as a motivator that is pushing you towards giving birth to a new and productive life. I know this is true for my own life.

A divinely prescribed pain is the dominant reason this book was created. In my life, I have been greatly blessed, but simultaneously, I have been stressed with a plethora of perplexing problems. I have experienced the extreme sickness of my son, desperate financial hardships, painful relationship setbacks, life-threatening medical and surgical emergencies. These experiences caused me to search for stress relief strategies that could help me to be productive despite my seasons of pain.

I will present strategies that will empower you to successfully cope with the anxieties of life. These strategies have drastically improved my level of happiness, joy, family satisfaction, level of income and strengthened faith. I am honored to share these stress relief strategies with you. This book contains eight main goals:

1. To help you learn strategies to strengthen your inner world, so that you can conquer all of the stress that exists in your outer world.
2. To help you discover the power of meditation. To maximize the stress management abilities you have within you.
3. To empower you to use your emotions to propel you to experience more happiness every day.
4. To provide health tips that will help you make physiological changes to reduce stress.
5. To show you how to attain and maintain your ideal level of happiness through problem solving skills.
6. To help you experience fulfillment by maximizing the potential of your personal and professional relationships.
7. To give you instant and executable action steps to decrease your level of stress despite the challenges you face.
8. To delineate physiological strategies to immediately eliminate excessive stress.

Let's discuss the effects of stress on the body. Excessive stress activates the fight or flight response in the body. This response is an automatic full body reaction to a perceived attack or threat to your survival. This reaction prepares you to defend yourself against danger. This response is a divinely designed action that is implanted in our brains. When your brain perceives that you are in danger it activates the central nervous system, then adrenaline, cortisol and other hormones are released into your blood stream. Your heart rate, blood pressure and breathing become elevated. Blood is rerouted from your digestive tract and directed to your muscles and limbs to provide you with extra energy and fuel to prepare to fight or flee. Your awareness of the surroundings becomes more intense.

In this heightened state, you could perceive almost anything as a possible threat to your survival. This physical response is a wonderful and powerful emergency defense system in life threatening situations.

The problem is that in our modern fast paced world, many people perceive almost anything as an emergency. Therefore, our fight or flight automatic reactions are over used in the body. When this happens, your brain perceives that you are experiencing a multitude of life or death emergencies every day.

If you perceive problems at your job, problems in traffic or problems in your home as immediate life or death situations, your body can over react and cause tremendous stress related health problems in your physiology. A recent study from the Center of Disease and Control showed that 11 out of the top 15 causes of death in this country are directly related to excess stress. Many things that stress us every day fully activate the fight or flight response and can cause us to over react to things that are not life threatening.

The buildup of stress hormones in our bodies can lead to physical pains, including headaches, chronic fatigue, depression, allergies, weaknesses in the immune system, hypertension and a host of other ailments. Therefore, we must take action immediately to improve our level of stress.

The following is a list of 10 things that I encourage you to do to maximize this stressforming experience and take action to balance your level of stress.

1. Be an active participant in the stressformer's process. What we do is what we really believe, the rest is just talk. Decide to be active and not passive while

reading this book. Take notes, highlight things, fold pages, fill in the blanks and write honest answers to experience tremendous change.

2. Focus on applying these strategies to your own life first. Many of the things you read may remind you of action steps that others should take to improve their lives; however, I ask you to, first, think of your situation and improve your life so that you can later help others. As many pre-flight announcements remind passengers on an airplane, "Parents if the oxygen masks fall due to an emergency, please put the oxygen mask on your own face, first, before your child's face" This is said because if you do not help yourself first, you will not be able to help anyone else.
3. Be brutally honest with yourself during this process. Do not sugar coat or beat around the bush while reading this book. Decide to take complete action.
4. Get partners to go through this process with you. You need positive people to encourage you during this time. No significant success is achieved alone.
5. Decide to finish this book. Medals are not given to those who start a race, but to those who finish. Decide you will complete this project.
6. Be proactive about your success. Do not hope for accidental or coincidental success. Take action to initiate definite success.
7. Prepare for a demolition. When old mindsets come up in your mind, decide that you will submit to this book which will demolish your old mindset. My family's favorite show is "Extreme Home Makeover". Before Ty Pennington and his team build a new house, they execute a demolition of the old house. For us to start a new life with a balanced level of stress, we have to

submit to demolishing the old mindsets, paradigms, and destructive ways of dealing with stress.

8. Read this book in small pieces. This is not the type of book you can just read through in a few days. Chew on the principles one small piece at a time. Give yourself credit for reading every day. Keep a good steady pace. Do the action exercises and you will get great results. Meditate and ponder about what you read.
9. Please send me an email to share your experiences, breakthroughs, paradigm shifts, and testimonies from reading Stressformers. Email us at stressformers@yahoo.com. Your testimonies will encourage me and provide all those who helped to make Stressformers a reality.
10. Have a lot of fun learning about yourself and gaining clarity on how to stressform your life.

Now it's time for us to get down to business and stressform our lives together. Thank you for taking this journey with me. I look forward to the stressformations that you will experience.

Chapter 1

The Day Everything Changed and Nothing Changed

"Get to the hospital emergency room immediately." Those were the chilling words from our Pediatrician after he examined our one year old son for only ten minutes. My wife and I nervously asked, "What's wrong? What did you find? Why do we have to go to the hospital, now?"

The Doctor in his rush to move us along ignored our questions, gave me a red ticket and said, "This will get you seen quickly. Please go now."

In a semi controlled panic, we rushed to the emergency room, gave the attendant the ticket and were rushed into an examination room. One thousand thoughts rushed through our minds, but we tried to be optimistic for each other and our son (A.J's sake).

#1. When life goes crazy, don't go with it.

They took us through the X-Rays, Cat Scans and exams quickly. Suddenly, two young doctors came in and broke the life changing news to us. The Doctor sympathetically whispered, "Mr. and Mrs. Jackson, your son has a condition called hydrocephalus. This means that there is fluid building up in his brain that is supposed to drain into the stomach, but in his case it's not. We need to operate on his cranium, immediately, to relieve the pressure and insert a shunt series machine that will drain the fluid properly. We must do this today, or he could die."

In a state of shock and disbelief we cried, said a prayer and gave consent for the surgery. After the five hour procedure, the rocedure went as planned and we were allowed to see our son.

I remember his eyes met ours as we walked into his room, while he laid in the bed looking at us; as if he just woke up from a nap with his pamper, white t-shirt, and half of his head shaven with his new beautiful four inch scar.

#2. Be thankful for the scars, because they remind you of your victories.

As we were preparing to take him home a few days later, the doctor met with us. As the physician explained to us how the shunt drains fluid from A.J.'s brain to his stomach, I remember thinking, "Thank the Lord. We are done with this process." Soon after that thought, the doctor made it clear that the shunt is a man-made machine that may last a month, a year or twenty years. But it would likely break down at some point, and we would have to bring our son back for another surgery. He also gave us a list of visible signs of shunt malfunction (such as sluggishness, lack of appetite and vomiting). He said we must quickly recognize these signs and bring him in to have the shunt replaced, or he would be in danger of losing his life. You can imagine the stress we felt after that five day ordeal.

For the next two weeks, we watched him every waking moment while living in terror that this machine would break down and what if we were not looking at him at that exact moment to recognize the malfunction? However, after many tears, talks and a two week period of normal activity from A.J, my wife said something that changed everything. She exclaimed," We can either spend every day in fear telling ourselves that this may be the day his shunt malfunctions, or we can resolve to be thankful for each moment we have with our son and daughter; while expecting each day to be wonderful. In that moment nothing changed, but everything changed.

#3. Nothing changed in his prognosis, but everything changed in our minds.

In the seven years since then, A.J has had surgery three more times, and we were right there to notice the signs and get him the help he needed each time. We are thankful that it has only been three times in seven years. Instead of focusing on the three days of surgery, we have decided to focus on the more than 2,500 days of health, he has experienced. We will discuss more about this in chapter 3.

#4. Instead of adding up your sick days, add up your healthy days.

Our life together is wonderful, because we don't waste time anticipating the worst. We expect the best.

#5. Instead of hoping you have a good day decide to create an extraordinary day.

I have learned many life changing stress relief lessons from this experience. Dr. Steven Covey said you should focus more on the things you can influence than on the things you're concerned about. It is best to focus your energy on the things you can change and expect the best regarding the things you can't change. I can't control whether or not the machine in our son's cranium works properly, but I can control whether or not the thoughts in my cranium work properly.

#6. We can't control what happens to us but we can control what we do about what happens to us.

As Dr. Wayne Dyer explains, "If you control your thoughts, you control your life." Notice he didn't say control what happens to you, but he said you can control your thoughts; and you control your response regarding what happens to you. In the moment you decide to take control of your response to the things that happen to you, everything will change inside of you even though nothing has changed outside of you.

Chapter 2

The Medication of Meditation

To meditate means to ponder, think about, muse, consider or to speak to oneself. Our level of stress is greatly influenced by our personal interpretation of life's events.

#7. It matters so little what others say to you, but it matters so much, what you say to yourself.

When you decide to structure your life around a positive mindset, there is nothing anyone can do to stop you. Conversely, when you decide to structure your life around a negative mindset, there is nothing anyone can do to stop you.

#8. Whatever you consistently visualize and verbalize, you will consistently materialize.

Therefore, meditation produces reality. You may ask how meditation can be prescribed as medication. Many health experts, including former Harvard Professor and M.D, Dr. Deepak Chopra has stated, "Our society is, too, heavily dependent on pills and over the counter medications and prescriptions." He advised that Meditation on positive thoughts produces the same amount of endorphins in the body as $1,000 worth of anti-depressant medication from your primary physician. Though there are certainly times in which we need to take prescriptions, many health experts say that many Americans are too heavily dependent on over the counter prescriptions to do what proper diet, exercise and meditation were designed to do. Many people are defeated in their minds. All success and failure regarding life's struggles start in the mind.

#9. The heart of the problem is the problem of the heart.

Many people believe what holds them back is a lack of finances, support or health, but countless success stories have been documented about those who have overcome adversities due to a positive mindset. There's a wonderful proverb, which says, "A merry heart does good like a medicine; but a broken spirit, dries the bones." By the heart, I mean the seed of the intellect where we think, reason and decide. This is of course, the mind. Not only do the scriptures affirm this, but many health experts agree and say that the mindset has a profound effect on leading a person to consistent health and wellness or consistent fatigue and sickness. Why? Your mind is so important. A merry heart can be the medicine to improve your health. Consistent thoughts of happiness, joy, excitement and a positive outlook on life can help and strengthen a person. Conversely, a negative and defeated mindset can actually hurt you physically, emotionally and spiritually.

#10. Make large daily mental deposits so you can make large daily mental withdrawals.

To produce positive thoughts, you should plant powerful and positive information into your mind. Utilize positive music, books, CDs, DVDs, poems, quotes etc. to inspire you on a daily basis. The body requires and receives daily fuel, so must the mind. BE PROACTIVE ABOUT PLANTING GOOD THINGS IN THE MIND. The eyes and the ears are the windows into your heart. Consistently look at and listen to things that are positive, empowering, encouraging, and strengthening to your spirit that will help you to visualize happy endings to your temporary problems.

Many people experience constant excessive stress because they allow the media, corporate sponsors and advertisers to tell them what to buy and how to think. Remember that advertisers' purpose is to sell products. To do that they must cause you to feel as bad about yourself as possible so that you will purchase their product to help yourself feel better according to their standards.

I have coached people who were dealing with depression. I have inquired, "What do you like to watch on TV?" One said, "Scary movies and murder mysteries." While another replied, "Cop shows." And they wonder why their financial life plays out like a horror movie. To avoid this, take the medication of meditation.

#11. Vision is more important than sight.

Your vision for your life is so important. The vision that we have will determine our destiny. I recently heard a story in which a reporter was walking through EPCOT with Roy Disney, the nephew of Walt Disney. The reporter relayed to Roy, "It's a shame that Walt did not live to see the opening of Disney World."

Roy Disney simply looked at the reporter and replied, "Walt saw it first; that's why you see it now." This illustrates the power of vision. Walt Disney had a vision for EPCOT. Since the vision was in his heart, it compelled him to complete his mission and bring the vision into reality. Our minds are so powerful. Access the power that is in your mind to help you relieve stress. Many believe that their mindset is a result of their experiences, but in reality your experiences are the result of your mindset.

#12. Your experiences are the results of your mindset.

A great motivator by the name of Brian Tracy commented, "The mind is so powerful that if you for twenty-one days say things to yourself out loud with faith, acceptance and belief, the thoughts will become your truth. Whatever you consistently say to yourself will eventually be accepted by your subconscious mind as truth." That reminds me of the scripture which reads, "As a man thinks in his heart, so is he." As you think, so you are. As you think, you become. Therefore if you are experiencing problems and struggles in your mind, in your heart or in your relationships, you have to envision positive results to your problems. Envision yourself rising above those situations with powerful and positive information that can help you overcome your obstacles. If you can see it, you can seize it. If you can envision it, you can have it.

As I said in chapter 1 about our son's illness, once we conceived the vision of health and wellness for him, everything changed. Our improved mental programming started to affect our outer world. When we began to focus on solutions rather than problems, our level of stress, not to mention his health, drastically improved. Sight shows us what is, but Vision shows us what can be. Helen Keller stated, "The only thing worse than being born without sight, is being born with sight, but without vision."

What holds many people back today from achieving their goals is not a lack of sight but a lack of vision.

Chapter 3

Question your Questions

Our lives and level of stress are greatly affected by our daily emotions. So much of what we do is not based on our ability or skills but on how we feel. Often, our emotions are signals that call us to take action to reduce stress. The most painful emotions we experience could be warning signals for us to make changes in our health, diet, amount of exercise or mental programming. If we heed these signals, we can utilize them to improve the quality of our lives at any given moment.

#13. We have the power to control our emotions.

What is the source of our emotions? Whether we give ourselves positive and/or negative feelings our emotions are determined by the principles we live by, and how we interpret and define life's events. What we feel is based more on our interpretation of our experience rather than on the experience itself.

#14. Question Your Questions.

One of the top Peek performance experts, Tony Robbins said, "Your emotions are greatly influenced by the questions you ask yourself. To experience better emotional balance in your level of stress, you must ask better questions. Focus determines feelings. Feelings affect emotions. Emotions drive your level of stress. Here are some better questions you can ask yourself when you are experiencing excessive stress. Please write the answers to these questions.

What are 2 things in your life for which you are thankful?

____

____

What are 2 good things you like about your JOB?

____

____

What are 2 great aspects of your MARRIAGE?

____

____

What are 2 advantages of spending time alone?

____

____

What are 2 things your children do well?

____

____

Name 5 body parts you couldn't live without, that are working well.

____

____

____

____

____

#15. Use positive questions to maintain an empowering focus.

How did you feel when you were writing those answers? Did you feel happy? Did you remember some things that made you laugh? The only thing I did was ask you the question, and you accessed the memory for yourself. You had these memories in your mind already. This is because questions determine focus.

#16. Better focus leads to better emotions.

I asked you empowering questions, and you came up with empowering answers, which caused and produced a great focus. When you're having severe struggles with your finances, health, emotions or relationships, you should have some great memories that you can access. Thinking back to happy memories will encourage you.

Chapter 4

Stressforming Health Tips

In the past, I believed that since I am a positive, upbeat, spiritual person, I don't have to be too concerned about my physical health. I was certain I could will my way into managing two full time jobs, my family, radio, prison, counseling, mentoring and training duties with no problem. I was wrong. Just one year before the writing of this book (due to excessive stress) I began to experience severe headaches, over-exhaustion and panic attacks.

During the onset of these symptoms I thought, "This can't happen to me. I don't believe in panic attacks or over-exhaustion." I was eating over the counter pills as if they were candy; but nothing helped. I knew I had to make serious changes in my lifestyle. I set out to do research on quick and inexpensive strategies to improve my physical health.

#17. Balance your physician's body of knowledge with your knowledge of your body.

You may wonder who approved this guy to give health advice. Well actually, I did stay at a Holiday Inn Express last night. So pay close attention to these tips. But seriously, I'm not a heath expert so you should consult your personal physician, fitness, and nutrition about your specific health questions. Combine these experts body of knowledge with your knowledge of your body to assess what's the best regimen for your body. These health tips have brought balance to my mental, physical and emotional stress levels so I offer these suggestions for your consideration.

#18. Laugh Out Loud.

Laughing is like inner jogging. When you laugh, your body relaxes; and the levels of stress hormones are reduced. Secondly, laughter sends neurological messages of happiness and joy to the brain. It also activates the release of health improving hormones such as endorphins, which act as the body's natural painkillers. To trigger a good laugh, I made a list of hilarious memories of family, friends, work events, movies and television shows that have cracked me up through the years. I think of those things when I need a quick stress relief minute. Write down 5 things about your family, friends and/or job that have made you laugh out loud.

____

____

____

____

____

#19. Take The Breath of Life.

Most people only take shallow breaths. This will increase stress in your body. Many health experts suggest taking deep breaths for at least five minutes twice a day will drastically decrease your level of stress. Inhale gentle breathes through the nose and exhale out through the mouth. If you don't purposely take deep breaths, you will feel sluggish and tired very often. Some believe when they feel sluggish, they need caffeine or an energy drink when in reality they need a healthy dose of the breath of life.

#20. Bring your heart and mind in sync through focus and breathing.

I recently heard about a study performed at the University of California, Berkley. According to the report the study was done to measure the electrical responses of your brain and your heart while stressed. It was found that the electrical responses are radically different between the brain and heart while under stress. A technique called "Heart Activation" was introduced. Subjects were asked to close their eyes and breathe in deeply and out slowly with their hand on their heart, or breathe in their heart for 3 minutes. The results showed this technique caused the electrical responses of the brain and heart to be in sync which caused the reduction of stress levels. When the case study participant's brain and hearts electrical responses were in sync they thought of effective strategies to help solve the problems that they were experiencing. What are two times a day you can schedule to do your breathing exercises?

____

____

#21. Improve your posture.

Many people sit and stand leaning forward, head down and with bad posture. This restricts your lungs and limits the amount of oxygen you can take into your body. If you stand and sit with your shoulders back, this will open up your sternum and rib cage which will allow you to breathe in more oxygen. This simple change in posture will reduce stress.

#22. Water is Life.

A few years ago, N.A.S.A developed drones to enter into Mars' atmosphere to search for life. To determine whether or not there was life on the planet, the drones #1 priority was to find Water.

Where there is water, there is life. Where there is no water, there is death. If the drone looked in your body, how much water would it find that you have put in it? Water is so important for life and vital to our management of stress. Studies show 60% of the population is dehydrated on a daily basis. It has been said that the first sign of dehydration is not thirst, but fatigue. If you feel tired most of the time, it's likely you need to drink more water. Water equals life for us and every living thing on our planet. The earth is 70% water; the brain is 76%; the muscles are 75%, and the bones are 25% water.

Water is a universal solvent that lubricates muscles, joints and helps to move metabolic waste. Peak Performance Expert, Tony Robbins says we should super-hydrating the body daily. To super-hydrate the body, he suggests that we drink half of our body weight in ounces every day. This will increase energy, help regulate blood pressure, and lubricate muscles. Drinking lots of water has also been known to assist in relieving headaches.

#23. Get proper Sleep.

A good night's rest makes the rest of your life easier. Dr. Keegan Sheridan reports that a recent survey by the National Sleep Foundation found that only twenty-eight percent of the people surveyed get at least eight hours of sleep per night. Insufficient sleep over time has been linked to fatigue, memory loss, immune system problems and depression. Here are some tips for optimal sleep.

A. Remove stimulants from your sleep area (silence cell phones, television, the computer and turn off bright lights).
B. Remove clutter from the sleep area. Don't use your bed as an office, entertainment area, paper filing area, lunchroom, clothing rack or bookshelf. Your sleep space should look and feel calm. Your brain will

interpret your bed only as a place to sleep, if you remove all other purposes from it.

C. Refrain from eating too close to bedtime. During sleep, your body is renewing itself and rebuilding cells. But when your body has to digest food while you sleep, the restful sleep and rebuilding process is interrupted.

#24. Take a weekly Sabbath day.

Everyone needs a day of rest. There was a time when I would do work almost every day. I talked to a Preacher friend of mine about doing some work on a certain day. But he said, "Sorry, this is my day off. I try not to do anything work related at least one day per week. It may be a different day each week depending on the schedule, but each week I take one day to rest."

I sighed, "WOW, I need to do that, too." Your mind and your body need a day of rest, at least one day a week. Many people do so much busy work all week that they are often thinking about sleeping, while they are trying to work; and thinking about work while they are trying to sleep.

Has this ever happened to you? Make time for rest. Dynamic rest is the basis for Dynamic activity, and Dynamic activity is the basis for dynamic rest. If you're not resting properly, then you're not working properly.

#25. Engage in Stress Reduction Hobbies.

Some great hobbies include golf, gardening, walking, running and listening to music. Whatever your chosen hobby might be, remember it can be used as a great stress reliever. Your hobbies should be activities that have nothing to do with your profession. It should be a tool that you can use to relieve stress.

#26. Your food effects your mood.

An area that also drastically affects your level of stress is your eating habits. We should all proactively design our daily diet with a good balance of vegetables, starches, fruits and vitamins. When you eat remember, life equals life and death equals death. You should work to eat more life (high energy) foods than death (low energy) foods. One important key is moderation. According to Dietary Expert and Author, Dr. Don Colbert, these foods take away energy and increase stress levels. Here are some food ingredients that produce bad health and increase stress levels.

Trans Fats. One Harvard Professor of Nutrition, Walter Willett, states," if Trans Fats disappeared from our country, there would have been 228,000 less heart attacks in 2007 alone." This is an ingredient in many of the most popular fast food items and snack products. The label that reads 0 grams of Trans Fats could mean that the item contains less than 1 Gram of Trans Fats as opposed to idea that the item contains noTran's fats.

Saturated Fats. Dr. Fuhrman calls cheese the single most dangerous food in America. This is due to its popularity, level of Saturated Fat and Casein.

Artificial Colors/Flavors. Sugars.

Salt and Sodium.

We should not only be concerned with what we eat, but how we eat. To further illustrate, I have identified eight types of eating styles that help put large quantities of unhealthy foods into our bodies.

1. The Martyr to the cause never leaves any food on the plate. He feels he must eat it all, even if he's full; because he doesn't want any to go to waste.

2. The Robotic eater eats while doing other things. She just keeps putting snacks into her mouth, while she's busy; and before you know it, she has eaten more than she intended.
3. Ms. Sensitive eats for comfort, connection and instant gratification.
4. Mr. Taste Tester consistently eats what he eats because of the taste and texture regardless of the level of nutritional value.
5. Mr. Roller Coaster fasts then pigs out. His body struggles to maintain balance.
6. The Fitness Fanatic counts every single calorie. This is the person who makes healthy eating very stressful for themselves and others around them.
7. The Nutrition Champion listens to her body and eats a well-balanced diet. She eats to live, she doesn't live to eat.

Which type(s) best describes you? To be a Champion, what changes will you make?

____

____

____

#27. Life equals Life.

Health Expert Anthony Robbins recommends you have 70% of your diet as green life giving foods. Living foods give more energy and decrease stress. Processed foods may fill you up but they do not provide fuel to keep your body going to your body to keep going.

#28. Use your senses.

Sights, Sounds, Taste, Touch, and Smell can heighten or reduce stress levels. How can you use your five senses to help instead of hurt? See things that you enjoy. Notice the smiles of beautiful children. When you're feeling down, look at pictures of vacations, weddings and happy family times in a photo album and remember the great feelings you had at those times. Pay attention to a beautiful sunrise, sunset and other examples of nature's wonders. The book of Psalms states, "The heavens declare the handiwork of God..."

There are so many things that you can hear that can help you feel better. You should hear sounds you enjoy by listening to encouraging music, children laughing, motivational messages or soothing recordings on CD.

You should smell things you enjoy. Whether it's potpourri, flowers or spices. The sense of smell is the strongest sense tied to memory. Since you will be reminded of many things through the sense of smell, use it to your advantage.

Use the sense of touch by hugging loved ones, giving and receiving pats on the back. Notice politicians as they greet many people at a rally. Many times they shake hands, pat the person on the back and look them in the eye to develop instant rapport and connection. Taste foods you enjoy. We certainly should eat healthy but many great tasting foods won't harm our health significantly if we enjoy them in moderation.

#29. Exercise moves tension out of the body.

Walking in sunlight for just twenty minutes a day improves your health significantly. What are three action steps that you can take to exercise more?

____

____

____

#30. Eat vitamins, vegetables and roughage.

Another great health tip is to consume more fruits, vegetables and multivitamins. This strategy has helped me to have more energy throughout the day. Instead of stopping for the typical fast food lunch, I now eat many veggie plates that taste great and cost about the same price as most burger value meals.

#31. Eat Breakfast daily.

It truly is the most important meal of the day. The purpose of this meal is to break the fast. You will have more fuel to help you through the day.

Chapter 5

Problem Solvers and Problem Revolvers

#32. Be a Problem Solver: Not a Problem Revolver.

Everyone has problems. Problems are a part of life and a major source of stress. The problems that have a profound effect on your level of stress include Financial, Emotional, Health, Relational and Spiritual. Furthermore, what determines your level of stress is not whether you have problems, but whether or not you believe you are able to solve the problems you have.

For example, if you have $500 worth of problems but at the same time you have $2,000 worth of solutions, you will not feel distressed. However, if you have $2,000 worth of problems and $500 worth of solutions, you may feel totally stressed out. In the midst of life's quandaries, you can choose to be a Problem Solver or Problem Revolver. Let's talk about one of history's greatest problem solvers.

I learned vital tools about being a problem solver while doing research for a Keynote Speech. I was scheduled to present during a Florida State Agency's Black History Program. The organizers requested that I include, in the speech, tools that would help staff members at all levels understand the importance of exhibiting leadership qualities and problem solving skills. I looked into the archives of African American History to research great figures to include in the keynote message. I wanted to find the most unlikely person who became a great leader despite seemingly facing insurmountable obstacles. Of the many possibilities, the leader I chose rose from one of history's most adverse calamities.

This problem solver was born in the 1820's on a plantation as a slave. This leader was illiterate and was consistently beaten so terribly that she developed seizures and lost partial sight in one eye. But despite losing her sight, she never lost her vision for freedom. This leader was Harriet Tubman.

During her teenage years, she became determined to find a way to escape slavery. She made two attempts with her brothers that were unsuccessful. She then decided the next time she would go alone. While the Fugitive Slave Law of 1850 (which permitted slave owners to kill runaway slaves without fear of indictment) resulted in the unjust capture and murder of many African Americans.

The law had a positive result the lawmakers never intended it to have. Many whites from the Northern states, who were previously indifferent about slavery, now were motivated to aid slaves who were trying to escape. Mrs. Tubman saw this as an opportunity to escape. Using only the North Star as her guide, she traveled over 400 miles to freedom. Most people today would hate to drive 400 miles, not to mention walk that distance. Moreover, nothing can stop a passionate problem solver.

This courageous Problem Solver turned her dream into reality without money, good health, family support, a car, a phone, Map-quest, Government Programs, State Legislation, a Grant, a Loan or the ability to read and write. So what's holding you back?

Later in life, she was a valuable aid in the Civil War. She also wrote a book about her life, and she stood up for women's rights. Harriet Tubman was an "Incredible Problem Solver".

Are you facing more adversity than this problem solver? Think about what Harriet Tubman accomplished without the human rights and technological advances we enjoy today. Also, think about what you and I can accomplish with them. As you know, Tubman returned many times to lead her family and many other African Americans to freedom. It has been said that she never lost one who was under her care. She is one of history's most incredible examples of how to be a "Problem Solver, not a Problem Revolver".

Here are eight lessons that we can learn from Harriet Tubman about Problem Solving.

1. Get angry about the current situation. That's right; get angry not just uncomfortable or upset. But you must get angry, if you're going to cause significant change. Needless to say, Mrs. Tubman got angry enough about slavery to overcome the odds and escape. Anger can be a great emotion, if we channel it into pursuit of a worthy goal without unjust treatment of others. Why are so many people settling for mediocre health, relationships and finances? One of the primary reasons is that most people aren't angry enough about the current situation to make the necessary changes. What are two things you are angry about in your life that you are committed to changing?

   ____

   ____

   ____

2. Develop Goal Lines. In football, the goal line represents the exact point where a player scores a touchdown. If you clearly define your goals and write them in order of importance, you will be very successful. Motivational Speaker Brian Tracy explained, "Action without planning is the cause of every failure." Before you make the plan, define the goal and don't move that goal. Many people are unsuccessful at hitting the bulls-eye of their goals, because the target keeps moving. Write your goals

down, because you can't hit a target that you can't see.

For example, write down your ideal weight. Write down exactly how much money you want to earn in the next 12 months. Write three characteristics of the ideal relationship with your mate?

____

____

____

3. What is the 'Why" behind your goals? Peak performance expert Tony Robbins stated, "Reasons come first, and answers come second." Ask yourself why do you want to lose weight? Why do you want a great relationship? Why do you want to earn $__________ per year? What will the accomplishment of the goal mean to you? The reasons for your goals will undergird you, as you work to turn your dreams into reality. It's very important to have moral and upright goals that will benefit not only you, but others. Harriet Tubman went back into the south nineteen times to rescue her family and others. I believe God helped her accomplish her goals despite seemingly impossible odds, because her reasons behind her actions benefitted not only herself, but many others. How will your financial goal achievement benefit your family? How will your spiritual goal achievements benefit your children? Describe the "Why" behind your goals in the Goal Line section.

____

____

____

4. Believe it's possible. Please answer these questions out loud.
   Has anyone ever risen from poverty to become financially successful?
   Has anyone ever lost 20, 50 or 100 pounds?
   Has anyone ever, drastically, improved his/her grades to graduate?
   Has anyone ever risen from abuse to have a joyful life? Has anyone ever reached the relationship goals you desire to reach?
   Has anyone ever reached the financial status you desire to reach?

   ____

   ____

   ____

5. Believe it's possible for ME. From the previous questions, we see that success is possible. But that does me no good, unless I believe it is possible for me. Many people believe success is possible for others, but they don't believe it's possible for them. My conviction is that if it's possible for anyone, it's also possible for me.

   *Abraham Lincoln was an orphan, reared in poverty, had two failed businesses and lost at least seven political the greatest Presidents in American History. **I BELIEVE I WILL ACHIEVE.**

   *Lucille Ball was told she had no talent and that she would never make it as an actor. Despite the discouragement, she became the star of I Love Lucy, **I BELIEVE I WILL ACHIEVE.**

*Walt Disney was fired from an ad agency, because they said that he lacked imagination. Then he created a mouse, a movie studio, theme parks and taught us all how to imagine. **I BELIEVE I WILL ACHIEVE.**

*Tyler Perry overcame physical and emotional abuse to become a great Actor, Producer, Writer and Movie Mogul. **I BELIEVE I WILL ACHIEVE.**

*Oprah Winfrey overcame abandonment, abuse and discrimination to become a world renowned talk show host and network owner. **I BELIEVE I WILL ACHIEVE.**

*Monique overcame criticism about her weight and discrimination to become an Oscar winner and talk show host. **I BELIEVE I WILL ACHIEVE.**

*Steve Harvey lived in his car for over a year. But through hard work and determination, he has become one of the world's premiere comedians. **I BELIEVE I WILL ACHIEVE.**

*Barack Obama persevered through the abandonment of his father and the death of his mother to earn a Harvard Law Degree, a U.S. Senate seat and the distinction as the first African American President of the United States. **I BELIEVE I WILL ACHIEVE.**

6. Develop a Game Plan. Now it's time to develop a strategic plan to solve your problem. The best Problem Solving starting point is to find a Mentor. When you want to lose 30 pounds, you should get advice from someone who has successfully accomplished that goal.

If you're highly stressed because of financial problems, you need a mentor who is successful in managing finances, even if you have to pay for their advice. You may say I don't know anyone who could mentor me, nor can I afford one. Don't be so sure of that. I have paid to secure the advice of many mentors I have never met. How is this possible? I have purchased books, C.D's, DVD's and searched their websites. I have learned priceless lessons from experts like Tony Robbins, Robert Kiosakee, Dr. John Maxwell, Dr. W.F Washington, Dr. Jack Evans, Delatorro L. McNeal, Wesley T. Leonard, Leroy Butler, Ivory L.Seright, Jimmy Ferguson, Eddie L. Harper and many others. By purchasing products from experts, I have received priceless advice in spirituality, finance, health, relationships, business and leadership in a fraction of the time at a fraction of the cost. So hire a mentor to help you develop a "Problem Solving Game Plan".

7. Adjust course. As you put your game plan into action, there will be times when you have to adjust course. Did you know that airline flights are off course at least 85% of the time? The reason they arrive at the planned destination is because the pilots understand the importance of adjusting course during the flight based on wind, cabin pressure, speed and altitude. Pay close attention to the relationship between your location and destination, as you are traveling toward your goals.

8. Never Give Up. In his book, The 21 Irrefutable Laws of Leadership, Dr. John Maxwell said that law number 15 is the Law of Victory. He stated, "A leader is not willing to accept defeat but will work

> diligently to achieve victory at all costs." Harriet Tubman refused to give up despite many obstacles and enemies. You may not achieve your goal on the first try. It may seem like you have failed, when you experience a setback. As Willey Jolley says, "A setback is just a setup for a comeback." Delatorro McNeal says, "Failure is not final; failure is feedback and fertilizer." Failure gives you feedback on how you should adjust course. It, also, fertilizes your efforts. Fertilizer (like failure) stinks at first, but it will eventually cause your dreams to flourish and grow.

Allow me to explain the concept of 'Problem Revolvers". Unlike Harriet Tubman and many other problem solvers who were committed to positive action, problem revolvers spend their time going around and around their problems. I call these people problem revolvers. Some believe that by thinking and talking about problems without action, they are helping the situation.

They remind me of a rocking chair. You can sit in it and have lots of activity, but you're not going anywhere. Whenever my wife and I have used rocking chairs, the purpose was to put one of our kids to sleep. Many people rock themselves to sleep instead of taking action to solve their problems.

Secondly, think of a Merry-Go-Round. It has lots of activity and nice music, but after it ends you are, basically, in the same spot you were when you started. When many people feel the pain of their problems, they immediately distract themselves from taking action by getting on their chosen Merry-Go-Round. Many activities are not wrong in and of themselves but when they are used as distractions and keep you from working to solve your problems, you will be rendered unproductive.

Here are a few examples of "Problem Revolver Merry-Go-Rounds".

Excess Television, Excuses, Blaming others, talking constantly about your obstacles in life without being productive.
Excessive use of Social Media sites that fail to help in goal achievement.
Over-eating, Drinking, Alcohol, Substance Abuses.
Excessive Sleep.
Pornography (Often an intimate relationship problem exists that's being avoided).
Constantly Borrowing Money (Often a result of a failure to budget, decrease spending and/or increase income)

What are three Merry-Go-Rounds you have used to feel better without actually making progress?

____

____

____

What are three Action steps you will take immediately to make progress in these areas?

____

____

____

Here are some reasons why people remain Revolvers for so long.

They use Softeners by convincing themselves things aren't that bad.
They Procrastinate
They say they're too busy
They assume it's too painful to try.
They profess there aren't enough resources
They believe they have no support
They operate with an ineffective strategy

Many believe if they give up they will avoid the pain of failure. In reality, the opposite is true. If you just give up without a fight, you're inviting the hurt, pain and failure automatically. We should fight hard for our dreams. We should fight hard to accomplish our goals. Shift from being a problem revolver to a problem solver. Develop a strategic plan to achieve your goals. You're not saving your strength or avoiding extra work by acting without a plan, it takes just as much energy and fuel to drive a car in circles as it does to drive it in a beneficial direction. Many hard working good people are running out of fuel driving in circles. Therefore, we should be diligent about designing a "Problem Solving Game Plan".

Benjamin Franklin exclaimed, "Do not leave till tomorrow what you can do today." Most people procrastinate and say, "We will work on our goals and dreams next week or next month." I say Work on them now."

#33. Every time you set a goal, do something immediately that will help you attain it.

This will produce momentum you will need to reach the goal.

#34. A pint of action is better than a pound of wishing.

Give yourself credit for every positive action. Some people are victims of the paralysis of analysis. They daydream and wish for things to get better but wishing is not enough. Take massive action and watch your wishes transform into realities.

#35. Even seemingly small steps in the right direction are still steps in the right direction.

Robert F. Kennedy emphasized, "Only those who dare to fail greatly can achieve greatly." Even if you work on your goals to make improvements in your health, relationships and finances; but you fall short at first, that's okay. You can learn something from it.

Oliver Wendell Holmes stated, “A moment’s insight is worth a life's experience.”

#36. Never quit.

Never give up, until you reach your destination. Never ever, ever give up. Dr. Maxwell in his tremendous book, “The 21 Irrefutable Laws of Leadership” included the law of victory. Victory at all costs. A great leader is not willing to accept defeat.

Chapter 6

Real-ationships and Relation-slips

According to many health experts, thriving intimate relationships are the most significant sources of stress relief. Conversely, bad relationships are the most significant sources of excessive stress. Therefore, we should be very interested in learning how to develop great relationships because we are hardwired to desire relationships. Follow these tips and you will develop real relationships, or real- ationships.

In the movie "Castaway", Tom Hanks was stranded on a deserted island, all alone. During this time, he became so desperate for any type of relationship. Finally, he found a soccer ball, dressed it up and started calling it Wilson. He talked to it every day. He even wept due to the guilt of being separated from his friend, Wilson who was in fact a soccer ball. He did this as he rode away from the island in hopes of returning to civilization. Why would a grown man talk to a soccer ball? The reason is we all desire relationships on some level.

Relationships come in different forms. These tips can apply to your relationship with yourself, the Creator, family, friends, co-workers or people you come in contact with even for a few moments. All could be categorized as relationships. Here are 10 keys you can use to improve your level of stress through the building of relationships with various people.

#37. Love unconditionally

Love is the oxygen of the soul. Love is defined as a choice; it's not always an emotional feeling of affection. It is a devotion that leads to willing, self-sacrificial service. If we treat others with love, we will experience a greater and more balanced level of stress. As the golden rule states, "Treat others the way you would have them to treat you." Love your family, love your friends, love those who are close to you, even love those who don't like you. Look for the good qualities in everyone. If you show love to them even when they do not show love to you, an emotion that could feel like hatred or animosity could be changed to be sadness and pity on those who mistreat you. Automatically, that emotion helps to relieve your stress. Hate, animosity, and resentment are stress-heightening emotions, but love will help you reduce your level of stress. You should walk in love for your mental, physical, spiritual and emotional well- being, even if your loving behavior doesn't seem to influence others to reciprocate.

#38. Be Patient with others

If you live with the mindset of being patient with everyone in your life, you will be able to reduce your level of stress. If you expect everyone to do everything your way, immediately without making mistakes, you're going to constantly feel stressed out. With patience, even if your relationships are not going the way you think they should go, things can turn around. Patience is defined as enduring afflictions over a long period of time with the view toward a brighter future.

#39. Pursue Paths of Peace.

Peace is defined as an inner calm; a disposition of calmness due to the confidence in your eternal spiritual realities. Inner calm helps reduce your level of stress. If you believe that everything is falling apart, everything is on you and you're not going to be able to get all of your assignments done, you will feel completely stressed out. Furthermore, if you live with peace and inner calm that comes from focusing on the big picture and eternal spiritual realities, you will experience a more balanced level of stress.

#40. Hold on to your Joy.

Joy is a pleasant disposition based on unchanging divine promises and eternal spiritual realities. Joy is much better than happiness. Happiness depends on what is happening, but one can have joy in spite of what is happening. In life, financial difficulties, sicknesses and many other painful things happen in life. If your joy is based on eternal realities instead of temporary conditions, you can look toward a brighter future despite the current problems you're facing in life.

#41. Be Human and Kind.

If you decide to treat everyone with kindness, you will avoid many stressful interactions. Kindness is defined as tender concern for others reflected in a desire to treat others gently. Kind words tend to turn away wrath, but grievous words tend to stir up anger. If you consistently treat others with kindness, it's very likely that others will treat you with more kindness as well.

#42. Give the gift of Forgiveness.

Forgiveness is releasing others of the debt that they owe you. You may ask how that can decrease my level of stress. If someone hurt you and they refuse to apologize, make it right or settle the debt; your conviction to hold on to that anger will hurt you far more than it would ever hurt them. Forgiveness helps you, even when it does not necessarily help others to improve. Forgiveness is releasing yourself from the prison of animosity with the key you have in your heart.

#43. Practice Self-Control.

Self-control is defined as restraining yourself from giving in to detrimental temptations that may hurt you and others you care about. One cannot engage in everything that (s)he carnally desires and expect to have great relationships. You should think about what you could lose by giving in to detrimental temptations. Use that as motivation to practice self-control.

Self-Control can also be described as patient submission in every offence and handling every relationship with care. Being gentle to others brings a calming mindset and disposition to most relationships.

Decide to live in faithful fidelity toward your loved one. This is loyalty and trustworthiness in action. If you are faithful to those whom you love, you won't have to experience the stress of hiding relationships, friendships, communications or the stress of hoping that you're not found out. The stress of betraying your loved ones can be dissipated by deciding to be faithful.

Moral excellence helps you practice self-control. Doing those things which you know are good helps to relieve your stress. One of the most stressful emotions is living in a way that is contrary to your conscience. That word, conscience, is made up of two parts, "con" and "science". Your conscience is contrary to science. It is that part of you that science cannot explain. It is that part of us that has a mental picture about what is good and what is bad. If we behave in a way that is good, we feel better about ourselves and our stress levels are reduced. But if we behave in ways that are bad, we feel bad about ourselves and that produces a heightened level of stress.

#44. The formulas of great relationships can work for anyone.

I would like to focus the remaining portion of this chapter on marital relationships. It has been said that a great marriage is the closest thing to heaven on earth, and a terrible marriage is the closest thing to hell on earth. Therefore, we should pay attention to tips that will produce great intimate relationships. The tips given are generalizations that reflect our society's relationship trends as a whole. These do not focus on individuals. There are individual exceptions to these rules. The tips given here will aid you in magnifying your intimate relationships.

Many people believe that there are some who are destined to have great marriages and some who are destined to have terrible marriages no matter what they do. This is not true. There is a formula to a wonderful marriage. All of those who are in bad relationships have to do is follow the formula to great relationships. For example, if I stumbled upon the recipe for making Kentucky Fried Chicken (even though I'm a bad cook) and simply follow the recipe down to the exact specifications, I could produce the same chicken as KFC (regardless of my talent, my ability, or my experience). If I follow the formula to create the Colonel's original recipe, I can produce the same product. Success in marriage works the same way.

Follow the formulas to great relationships and watch them be transformed forever.

#45. Recognize that relationships are ever growing and changing.

It's not something that is a fixed state and time. It's constantly developing, and it's never ending. Some people want to work on their relationship for a few days or a week and want it to get better, and they want to be done working on that to move onto something else. Great relationships are ever developing, growing and changing regardless of how great it is today. If you neglect it for the next three months, your relationship could die. You could have a healthy relationship, if you accept the fact that it will change for the better or for the worse depending on the consistent level of nourishment that is invested into it.

Relationships are designed to constantly grow and develop. If you view your relationship as something that is fixed, unchanging, doing okay or not in need of attention, your relationship will not thrive. Everything that is living on this earth must grow, or it will die. Humans must grow or die. Plants must grow or die. Animals must grow or die. Everything that is living will either grow or it will die. Relationships are the same way. Relationships are designed to constantly develop, increase, grow and magnify the human experience. Your relationship needs consistent attention.

#46. Appreciate the fact that men and women are different.

Masculine	**Feminine**
Tend to be more Goal Oriented	Tend to be more Process Oriented
Tend to be more singularly focused	Tend to be more able to multitask
Tend to connect through competition	Tend to connect through communication
Tend to crave credit from loved ones	Tend to crave connection with loved ones
Tend to desire more time alone	Tend to desire more time together
Tend to focus more on the big picture	Tend to focus more on intricate details
Desire to do big things for the spouse	Tend to say the little things mean so much
Tend to be happier when doing a good job	Tend to be happier while sharing feelings While loved ones actively listen
Tend to desire to solve problems alone	Tend to desire to solve problems together
Tend to focus on the (perceived) facts	Tend to focus on the (perceived) feelings

The emotional, physical and psychological differences that exist between men and women were not meant to be tolerated, but celebrated. Despite the divine design, many men and women are stressed out due to our differences. Often men give in relationships what men need. Many women give in relationships the things that they need. However, we should accept and appreciate the fact that men and women have different emotional needs. They have different ways of dealing with stress. If you expect your mate to think, react and deal stress the exact same way that you do, you will never be happy.

In other words, men and women are different. Accept this fact and appreciate this fact. Your mate was given to you as a compliment to you. Think about the combination of Kool-Aid and sugar. These are different properties that come together to form something better than they could ever be separately. The sooner you accept and appreciate the fact that your mate is different from you and always will be, the sooner you will have a better level of stress.

#47. Strive to bring out the best characteristics of your mate.

Accomplishments are achieved many times by bringing two or more different people with different talents together to achieve common goals. This is one of the main purposes of relationships. For example, in the game of football, the quarterback, the running back, the lineman, and the receivers all have different talents, but they can achieve common goals, not by trying to change the talents of those in other positions. This takes place by utilizing all the individual talents for the common good.

In music, singers, guitarists, drummers, pianists and producers all have different talents, but they work together to produce a product that can bring benefits to everyone. In a choral group, sopranos, altos, bass can sing at these different levels. Individually, they sound good; however, collectively, they sound wonderful. Therefore, if we strive to bring out the best characteristics of our mates, we can achieve great things together. No great success is achieved alone. Even solo artists need many people working behind the scenes to help them achieve their goals. So it is in our relationships. We must remember that we are much better together than we could ever be alone.

#48. Wives, remember your husband wants a cheerleader.

In sports, many players are on the field of play at the same time, and on the sidelines they have cheerleaders who cheer them on to victory. Every man wants his mate to be his greatest cheerleader. The cheerleaders smile; they dress nice, in ways that appeal to him. When he does something good, they are very animated, cheering and shouting and saying encouraging things to him. But when the player or the team does something bad, cheerleaders are silent. They don't ridicule the players. They are overly vocal and animated over positive things, but very hesitant and quiet over negative things. Wives, if you become his greatest cheerleader, he will likely be motivated to work extra hard to be better for you and for himself.

#49. Husbands, remember your wife wants a knight in shining armor.

Many of us have seen the movies of the damsel in distress and a knight in shining armor coming to rescue her. Many women want a knight in shining armor. Women are able to achieve goals just like men but they want a man to put her feelings, desires and needs before his wants. The only difference is from what does she wants to be rescued. That's your job as a man. You will need to research and find out from what it is that she needs to be rescued. Don't get angry about it; don't tell her to get over it; and don't discount her feelings with what she's struggling. Rescue her. That is your avenue of becoming the hero. Once you rescue her, it is like you have opened her heart. A woman's heart is like a vault. If you learn the combination, use it. You can open the door and receive the benefits of all the treasures inside.

#50. Many men feel a desire to get close to a woman, and then they desire to spend time alone.

This is a natural process. Men use this "in and out" movement process. He will get close to a woman, spend time with her, but then he also wants time to himself to go into his 'man cave", to think, relax and work on his hobbies. That's okay. Ladies, please give your men time in his cave or with his friends and he is likely to naturally return to you. But some women crowd their man, because they want to be together more than him. This is not healthy. Give him that time to himself to go into his "man cave". If you do that, he'll come back and be passionate to you in due time.

#51. Show concern for your wife during her natural ups and downs.

There are days when your woman may feel great, excited and happy and cheerful. There are days when she feels very sad and down. This is a natural process. Sometimes men try to stop their women from feeling bad. Don't try to stop her or criticize her for feeling bad. Be there for her, listen to her, validate her feelings and let her know that she has a right to feel the way that she feels. In the process of time, she will naturally bounce back from her downtime and come back up again. But if you criticize her for feeling down, she will be down even longer and possibly be very upset with you.

#52. When many woman talk about her problems, we shouldn't expect her to always cheer up quickly.

Many times men who listen to their women and try to support them emotionally, wants her to cheer up, immediately. Sometimes this will not happen. Give her the time and space and validation to feel, and she will bounce back up. Just as a man needs his alone time to bounce back into the relationship; a woman needs her downtime to bounce back into feeling better.

#53. Give him time in his cave.

Many men have a natural desire to sometimes go into their cave. If you give him this time, he will likely come back to you renewed and refreshed.

#54. Husbands, plan a date far in advance.

I've been guilty of trying to take my wife out at the last minute. One evening I was about to get off of work, I just felt like taking my wife out. I called her and said, "Let's get a babysitter, and let's go out tonight." I thought she would be very excited, but she seemed to be even more stressed. She said, "Oh no. I planned to do A, B and C. Now, this will change my plans." I learned the best and most romantic way to plan a date for my wife is to plan it far in advance. Of course, women and men like to be spontaneous, sometimes. If you plan a date a week in advance, women mentally think about it, feel good about that upcoming date and the thought builds up anticipation.

#55. Husbands, work to be less distant.

Many men, as they think deeply about the problems of life, want to spend time alone. Often a man does not want to discuss a problem until he has decided what action he decides to take to solve it. During his thinking process he may not realize how distant he seems to his wife. She often knows there is a problem that's on his mind, even if she doesn't know what the problem is. This will cause her excess stress and she may cause him excess stress as she tries to find out what's wrong. Work to include her in more of your thought processes. She is your helper and aid. If you let her know about the problem you are pondering she will likely unite with you against the problem. Nothing draws people together like problems. A husband will either let his wife know there is a problem or he will become the problem. Take your pick. Let her know that she is making a positive difference in your life and that will help reduce her stress.

#56. Wives, work to be less talkative.

Women, many times, have a natural instinct to talk and verbalize their feelings. They often don't realize how much they actually say. It's good to share your feelings, but sometimes, in talking to your man make an effort not to talk so much. Listen to him talk without interrupting him or criticizing his point of view. This will help him feel that he is being heard and appreciated. Mutually decide on a convenient time to talk. If you say the dreaded words, "We need to talk" he might give a negative response but don't be discouraged. Ask him to schedule a time to talk. It doesn't always have to be right now. During the discussion both sides should try to have an equal amount of time to share their thoughts and feelings without rebuke for feeling the way they feel. This will help both feel more comfortable with sharing their feelings.

#57. Many women give too much to others at the detriment of her.

Many women give so much and they expect their mate to give back to them. According to Dr. John Gray, author of Men Are from Mars, Women are from Venus, "A man should not be held responsible for making a sad woman happy, but he should be held responsible for making a happy woman happier." Women who are in need of emotional support should spend more time doing activities that will give them support instead of giving so much to others. Often women give so much to their loved ones and expect them to instinctively reciprocate. When this doesn't happen she often feels disrespected, ignored and emotionally drained. I can't promise your husband or your children will give you the support you feel you need. Give yourself the stress relief help you're waiting others to give to you.

Here are some powerful stress relief strategies you can give to yourself.

#58. Look in the mirror and say to yourself, God loves you so much and so do I.

#59. Look in the mirror and tell yourself five things you love about you.

#60. Pamper yourself. Get your hair done, manicure and a pedicure.

#61. Talk to positive loved ones on the phone.

#62. Re-read notes, cards etc. that have encouraged you through the years.

#63. Listen to your favorite music.

#64. Take a scented bath and relax.

#65. Shop for fun with a positive friend.

#66. Look in a photo album filled with pictures of loved ones.

#67. Do something for people who have less financial wealth & health.

#68. Spend time with babies and small children. They are stress relief experts.

#69. Read the Bible's statements about what God thinks of you.

#70. Read poetry and write a journal of your thoughts, feelings and goals.

#71. Go to a movie alone. Eat popcorn, laugh and enjoy yourself.

#72. Take an online class in a hobby you enjoy.

These are just a few ways women can relieve their own stress without waiting for someone else to offer their assistance.

Now it's time to talk to the men. There are many men who are loving, caring and considerate of their wives, children and their families. I believe thousands of men who are committed to their families do not receive the credit they deserve. To those men, I honor you. I commend you for your commitment. Keep up the good work.

There are some men who feel they have tried and failed to please their wives. As a result of their perceptions of past failures, they have decided to give up on attempts at improving their relationships. I want to focus this section on how men can create an environment that leads to a happier wife and a happier life.

With simple changes in your strategies, you can drastically improve your relationship. Think of it this way. What should a football team do that is having trouble running the football on the opposing team? Should they give up or should they keep adjusting their strategy until something works? You know the answer.

Here is a list that can help men to drastically improve their relationships.

#73. Little things mean so much. As men, we want to do great big things for our wives like take her on vacations or shopping sprees. Women enjoy those things, as well. But remember, men, little things mean so much. Some men believe they'll do something very big or nothing at all. Instead of trying to do some big thing for her every few weeks, do the little things she likes every day. Relationship expert Dr. John Grey advises that from the woman's perspective, "every act of love scores just about equally with every other act of love." For example, I know my wife gets just as excited about my compliments, offers to do the grocery shopping and cleaning the kitchen as she would about going to a restaurant or receiving a dozen roses. So instead of waiting to do something to make her happy that costs lots of money, I can get the same reaction from her by helping with household duties. Why? Little things mean so much.

#74. Ask her specific questions about her day. Practice listening to her with the sole intention of respectfully understanding what she's going through without offering quick solutions. That's right; you don't always have to have all the answers. Just listen and pay attention. If she feels you are actively listening while she's talking, and working out her feelings, she will feel better even if you don't have the answers to her problems.

#75. Offer to help with projects she is working on.

#76. Compliment her hair, smile and outfit. She wants to know what you think.

#77. Hug and kiss her first thing in the morning, when you separate & reunite.

#78. When you're going to be late, let her know your location and arrival time.

#79. Make a CD of her favorite songs.

#80. Give her a massage without asking for something in return. She'll reciprocate when you least expect it.

#81. Plan a romantic evening out weeks in advance. Give her plenty of notice the date is coming. She will get excited every time she thinks or talks about the date to her girlfriends.

#82. Give her one rose twelve times instead of giving her twelve roses once.

#83. Fix things that are broken around the house without being asked.

#84. Schedule a consistent date night that can't be missed.

#85. Thank her for loving you and the family.

#86. Compliment her often for juggling her family and her career with grace.

#87. Be responsible for preparing at least one dinner per week.

#88. Continue to remind her that you will always take care of her and the family. Assure her that she can always feel safe in loving you because of your love for her.

#89. Compliment her often on the beautiful home she has created.

#90. When you're stressed, do things for the people you love.

Just as women have a hard time when they're under stress doing things for themselves, men often have a hard time doing things for others when they are stressed out. During times of high stress, women should focus more on doing things for themselves, because they spend so much time doing for others. Conversely, during times of high levels of stress, men should focus on doing things for others, because they generally spend time doing things for themselves. Men generally relieve stress by doing, while women generally relieve stress by communicating. Through these activities, men can improve the level of stress for themselves and their significant others.

Chapter 7

I am Blessed to be Stressed

I have said many times, “I am too blessed to be stressed.” From this point of view I believed being blessed meant that you are not stressed and being stressed meant that you are not blessed. Through life experiences, study and contemplation I have come to realize you can be blessed and stressed at the same time. The word blessed comes from the word which means one has favor, joy, commendation and consecration from God. Blessings have a spiritual focus but also positively affects the blessed person’s physical existence. The blessed one is fully satisfied with eternal spiritual realities and is not dismayed by temporary physical circumstances. The word stressed gives the idea of the state of dynamic tension created when we respond to perceived demands, pressures and threats. Often our blessings come to us with stressors attached.

> If you’re a blessed person who has a family, you’re also stressed by family.
> If you’re a blessed person with a job, you’re also stressed by the job.
> If you’re a blessed person with a business, you’re also stressed by the business.
> If you’re blessed to be a strong person, you’re stressed by others who depend on you.

You can either focus on the fact that you are stressed, or focus on the fact that you are blessed. I choose to focus on the blessing and accept the stressing that comes with it. I would much rather keep my family than lose them and the stress of caring for them. I would much rather keep my job than lose it and the stress that goes with it. If you pay attention, you will find in every stressful circumstance there is a blessing hoping to be discovered and appreciated. There are many positive aspects to stress. As the saying goes, no pain, no gain. My mess has become a powerful message. Your frustration is designed to lead you to evaluation, application and celebration. In other words, I am blessed to be stressed and so are you. Here is a list of helpful tips about the positive effects of stress.

#91. Stress teaches you to reach out to the Lord for help to maintain your joy.

#92. Stress teaches you to examine your actions, beliefs and strategies.

#93. Stress inspires you to reach out to positive friends for guidance and support.

#94. Living with Faith turns every stressing into a blessing.

The Patriarch Abraham was commanded by God to leave his home land in Genesis 12:1. This father of the faithful took his wife, nephew and his possessions to search for a promised land. He was stressed but focused on the fact that he was blessed. Many today are stressed with uncertainty regarding employment, income and health concerns. Abraham literally walked by faith, not by sight. He believed in God's ability more than his inability. He was fully persuaded that God was able to perform that which he promised. This level of faith is necessary for us to live a blessed life.

#95. Living with Integrity turns every stressing into a blessing.

Joseph, the son of Jacob, suffered through the stress of being betrayed by his brethren, sold into slavery, falsely accused of sexual harassment and years of imprisonment. Despite his trials, Joseph kept his integrity. The stressful circumstances actually put him in position to be blessed with a promotion to the position of second ruler in Egypt. The Lord used his stress to navigate him into the perfect position to save the lives of the Hebrews and the Egyptians from starvation during a devastating famine. Joseph testified in Genesis 50:20 "....what you did you meant for evil but God meant it unto good..." Instead of focusing on the stressing he went through, Joseph focused on the blessings God brought him too.

#96. Living with Patience turns every stressing into a blessing.

The book of Job is a stress relief manual. Here are some examples of Job's stressful storms of life. Job experienced death stress when all ten of his children died in one day. He experienced financial stress when he lost all of his financial wealth. He experienced health stress when he was afflicted with boils all over his body. He experienced relationship stress due to his wife and friends complaints. Keep in mind all of these calamities happened simultaneously. Yet this stressed man remembered he was a blessed man because of his relationship with God. Notice a few of Job's victorious quotes during his troubles.

> "...What? Shall we receive good at the hand of God and not also receive (suffering) evil." (Job 2:10)

> "...though he slay me, yet will I trust in him." (Job 13:15)

> "...all the days of my appointed time I'll wait until my change comes." (Job 14:14)

"I know my Redeemer lives…." (Job 19:25).

"But he knows the way that I take, when he has tried me, I shall come forth as gold." (Job 23:10).

After he suffered the Lord rewarded his faithfulness by giving him double for his trouble. He also testified now I SEE YOU LORD (Job 42:5) he was blessed with a clearer picture of God. What a blessing. What are you willing to go through to see God more clearly?

Job recognized he was stressed, but he held on to the faith that he was also blessed. We must remember even in the midst of feeling stressed, we are still blessed.

#97. Following true north moral principles even when it hurts turns every stressing into a blessing.

Many people have no problem doing the right thing as long as they can avoid pain. Living according to ideals that are consistent with moral principles is sometimes painful. Whether it's giving money back to the waiter who gave you too much change or giving up smoking, doing the right thing is sometimes painful to the body but it feels great in your soul. Live consistently with your conscience and you will likely decrease your level of stress. Many psychological experts agree that a person is stressed the most when they consistently live in violation of their conscience. Some have a desire to do the things that are consistent with their conscience, but due to pain they fail to do what's right. For example, a person who has been addicted to drugs, alcohol, smoking or gambling may truly want to quit, but quitting involves a high level of pain. Letting go of destructive habits is met by most of the public with attention, admiration and respect. People who are faithful in marriage, honest, consistent and/or quit doing drugs are highly respected for their accomplishments. Do the right thing even when it hurts and you will be happy you did.

Chapter 8

Storm Chasers

I recently heard a radio talk show episode in which the host interviewed a man who said he was a storm chaser. These are people who chase hurricanes and tornadoes. When hurricanes hit a particular area, the chasers spring into action. The chasers travel toward the storm while everyone else runs and hides from the storm. During the interview, the host asked questions that I would have asked "Are you crazy? Were you dropped on your head as a child? Are you a daredevil or a thrill seeker? Do you have a death wish?"

This man politely listened to the host and answered her individual questions. He then said something that amazed me, "Our main goal in chasing the storms is certainly not to be thrill seekers or have fun; we chase the storms from a safe distance to study the travel patterns and characteristics of the storms to better prepare for future storms." To add, he explained, "Our research helps weather experts predict the power and the path of storms. Architects use our findings as they build weather-resistant buildings and structures which will withstand future storms. Furthermore, our research helps city officials, policemen, firemen, and ambulance staff to prepare, aid and assist those in need. The information gathered during our research concerning the speed, strength and the path of the storms is extremely important."

I was amazed. While many people run from the storms, these individuals chase and study the storms. At that moment I decided to become a storm chaser. I don't mean that I will ever purposely drive towards a hurricane. I decided to research the storms in my life to learn the lessons from them and prepare for future storms. I've learned that it is important to study the storms of life and examine my reactions during the storms and realize areas in which I can improve.

You can stressform your life by becoming a Storm Chaser. In every storm of life, whether it is financial, relational, emotional, physical or spiritual, lessons can be learned. Study your storms. In many storms of life most people run, look for a hiding place, or just ride out the storm hoping that it will end soon. Very few people study why they have relationship problems. Very few people study how they can get out of the financial or health storms that they are facing. However, if you are going to stressform your life, you have to become a storm chaser. I believe that the Word of God gives us vital tools on how to be effective storm chasers. In every storm, we should be more concerned with what we can do in the storm that is under our control as opposed to things that are outside of our control. There are many lessons that I have learned from examining my storms. Here is a list of some of those lessons.

#98. Stressful storms should be expected.

One of the greatest protections against the anxiety of storms is to expect storms. I live in Florida, a state known for experiencing many hurricanes. Every hurricane season, the weather channel reports the possibility of major storms. Daily, we live with that possibility, but we continue living our lives while focusing on preparing for the storms. Some say, "Why don't you move away?"

My response is, "No matter where you live there will be storms. Even if we traded in the storms of Florida for the snow and blizzards of the northern U.S, the Tornadoes of central U.S, the earthquakes of western U.S, the famine's of some parts of Africa, or Tsunami's of Japan, we would still experience storms." Stressful storms should be expected.

The question is how will you react to the storms. We are responsible not for the action, but for our reaction to life's storms. I can't control the storms. I am able to control my response to the storms of life. Whatever you expect cannot completely depress you. Many are depressed by their stressful storms, because they believe they are not supposed to experience storms. There is power in expecting that there will be storms in life. In our cars, many of us ride around with umbrellas, because we expect rainy and stormy days to come. The best thing we can do is prepare for the storms.

In Matthew chapter 7, Jesus talked about two houses. He stated both houses were attacked by storms. The rain descended, floods came, and wind blew on both houses. Rains identify storms from above. Floods identify storms from beneath. Winds identify storms from all around. The difference is that one fell, and one house did not fall. Why? Because one was founded on the rock, and one was founded on sand. If we build our houses on the solid rock, we can survive any storm. Expectation and preparation are two of the greatest protections against the anxiety of storms.

#99. Stressful storms are temporary.

In 2004, the state of Florida experienced four very powerful hurricanes. During some of those hurricanes, our home's electricity went off. We went through weeks of severe rain, thunder, lightning and wind damage. I was secluded with my family in our dark and humid home. But one thought comforted us in the midst of those tremendous storms. We knew that those storms were temporary. We were certain that those storms could not last. Can you imagine if someone is in the midst of a hurricane or tornado believed the storm would last for five years? You would tell them this may be a bad storm, but it is temporary. So it is with the stressful storms. Remember, it's temporary. Every storm has a shelf life, because it cannot last.

The wise King Solomon said in Ecclesiastes 3, "There is a season to everything under the sun." Everything is temporary, except God. Only God is eternal. Every circumstance is temporary in this world. Therefore, we should have the faith that storms are temporary. You can outlast the storm. That's how you defeat stressful storms that you cannot change. Focus your efforts on preparing for the storm, enduring the storm and outlasting the storm.

#100. Stressful storms produce change for the better.

Storms are intended to cause us to grow and change for the better. As we said, Jesus our Lord, in Matthew chapter 7 talked about those two houses. One fell, because it was founded on sand. One did not fall, because it was founded upon a rock. Notice the purpose for the storms. The storms came, not to destroy the house, but to prove to you and others what your house is built upon. Your storms did not come upon you to destroy you, but to prove to you how powerful your foundation is. There is very little growth in good times. There's very little advancement or change for the better during times of peace. However, there is much change and growth during times of storms. Never trust a faith that has not been tested. Your faith is only as strong as the test it is able to withstand. The level of your strength is based on the storms you are able to successfully endure.

Whenever God wanted to do a great thing, he caused or allowed a stressful storm to occur In the life of his servants. Look at David in First Samuel 16. David was a shepherd boy in Jesse's house. Jessie sent David to take food to his brothers. David went to the battleground and saw the stressful storm of the giant, Goliath who challenged God's people. With God's help, David showed great character development by faithfully deciding to fight the giant. He fought and defeated the giant. Soon after he was promoted.

Stressful storms are God's prelude to promotions. Daniel in the Lion's Den was a stressful storm. The book of Daniel says a ruling was instituted in Babylon that no one could pray to any diety except the king's god for thirty days. Daniel prayed to his God with his window open as he always did. He was arrested, brought before the king and thrown into the den of hungry lions. God protected Daniel in his temporary den of stress. After Daniel came out of that stressful storm, he received a promotion. Stressful storms produce change for the better. You cannot become who you are supposed to be, unless you are willing to go through stressful storms.

#101. Stressful storms should be managed.

God created us to be excellent managers. God will never allow growth without proper management. Whatever you mismanage, you will loose. If you mismanage your health, you will loose it. If you mismange your money, you will loose it. If you mismange your marriage, you will loose it.

If we properly manage the things that God has given us, we will have more growth. We should pray for guidance in management. If we properly manage the stressful storms in our lives, God will automatically produce growth. Stressful storms should be expected. They should be considered temporary events. They produce change for the better, and they are tests of our ability to manage life's storms. Thank God for stressful storms.

Conclusion

Congratulations, you did it. You've finished the Stressformers book. What an honor this has been to share this experience with you. Just as experiencing this book has been a journey for you, writing it has been a tremendous honor and incredible journey for me. I am certain that you have experienced stressforming paradigm shifts, happiness, empowerment, peace, encouragement and strength from reading these pages. As you move forward from this book, please allow me to challenge you to do the following:

1. Daily, go back and re-read parts of this book. As you continue on in life, you will grow and face more and more challenges. The pages, quotes and statements in this book were designed to help you, not just for a few days or a week or a month, but for the rest of your life. Continue to be reminded of the stressforming strategies you have read about in this book. Please don't loan this book out to anyone. Most of the time when you loan books out, you don't get them back. Inform people (if they ask you for your copy), "No, my friend. You have to get your own copy. This book is mine."
2. Apply what you have learned to your daily life. Throughout this book you have learned a multitude of tips and strategies that will empower you to live a balanced life. Now, it's time to apply what you have learned. As you continue to apply these principles to

your life, read many other sources about stress relief. Search for information on the web, read other books, blogs, newspaper, magazine articles, etc., that teach powerful information about stress relief. If you feel the need, secure the services of a counselor or a coach to help you continue to grow in stress management.

3. Remember to send me an email at stressformers@yahoo.com to inform me of the ways this book has changed your life. Your personal story about the impact this book has had on your life will help me and many others stressform our lives now and for years to come. Visit my website, stressformersllc.com, to give us feedback about the book.
4. Teach others about this book and its impact on your life. You don't truly learn something, until you teach it to others. If this book has helped you in many ways, don't keep it a secret; tell your family, friends, co-workers and neighbors about the impact Stressformers has made on your life. Encourage as many people as you can to Stressform through the principles you have learned.
5. Consider this day as your commencement. Now that you have finished this book, you will start a new season in your life. Remember the word commencement, that describes graduation ceremonies, does not mean the end. It actually means the beginning. To commence means to start. When students graduate, it's actually the start or the commencement of a new season of life. Now that you, the student of Stressformers (the book), have graduated, you can commence to live an empowered life and encourage others to do the same.
6. May the blessings and favor of God be upon your every endeavor as you travel on your journey.

www.ingramcontent.com/pod-product-compliance
Ingram Content Group UK Ltd.
Pitfield, Milton Keynes, MK11 3LW, UK
UKHW040557210726
13854UKWH00007B/1372